SHATTERED SOULS

SHAY SOLACE

Shattered Souls
Copyright © 2024 by Shay Solace.

All rights reserved. No part of this publication may be reproduced, distributed, or transmitted in any form or by any means, including photocopying, recording, or other electronic or mechanical methods, without the written consent of the publisher. The only exceptions are for brief quotations included in critical reviews and other noncommercial uses permitted by copyright law.

MILTON & HUGO L.L.C.
4407 Park Ave., Suite 5
Union City, NJ 07087, USA

Website: *www.miltonandhugo.com*
Hotline: *1-888-778-0033*
Email: *info@miltonandhugo.com*

Ordering Information:
Quantity sales. Special discounts are granted to corporations, associations, and other organizations. For more information on these discounts, please reach out to the publisher using the contact information provided above.

Library of Congress Control Number:	2024923493
ISBN-13: 979-8-89285-375-0	[Paperback Edition]
979-8-89285-376-7	[Hardback Edition]
979-8-89285-377-4	[Digital Edition]

Rev. date: 11/19/2024

Dedication

To those who wish they weren't here but still are, this is for you.

A heavy heart once severed from its truth.
Here lies the hollowed-out hope torn away.
Bloody and bruised, with no more of its youth,
Stomped on, stranded, then buried to decay.

Love is a futile, fickle fantasy.
The cause of death: betrayal, broken trust.
Alone, abandoned, left with naught to see,
A new reality, feeling unjust.

Yet, through the silence, whispers start to grow.
Whispering promises of happiness,
The fleeting feeling of fear now shallow,
Soft echoes of a future, bright and fresh.

Though shadows linger, a spark now ignites.
A warm whisper of hope to guide a light.

Daddy Issues

Pursuing relationships I can't commit to.
Loving you might give me value.
Easy for you to undo,
All of me when you blow your fuse.
Suppressing everything in case you withdrew.
Eager to keep you, not caring if I'm used.

Leave, and I'll have nothing to lose.
One of us is red, the other turning more blue.
Violet, the prettiest bruise.
Endlessly chasing, yet you couldn't pursue.

Me, you didn't choose.
End of us, but the cycle still continues.

My Life In Five Stages

Denial is a funny thing.
So funny that even if I'm told I'm in denial, I'd ignore that truthly sting.
Because there is no way that this is happening.
There is no way I'm ready for the sorrow that the truth will bring.

But it is really happening, and now all I feel is dread.
All I see is red.
Red, hot, simmering anger fills my heart and head.
Masking my true emotions I wouldn't dare to shed.
Too many terrible things have been done and said.

Now I'm overthinking of what could have been.
Suddenly, I find myself bargaining.
Could've, should've, would've scenarios begin.
But no fake scenario would ever win.

Nothing would have worked and it certainly does not matter anymore.
What's the point if I can't go back to before?
Nothing would be able to restore
My bleeding heart and bloody corps
Do I even have anything to live for?

But I have to move on.
Even when it hurts, I need to be strong.
Because to hurt means I have loved a ton
And for that, I am grateful to have lost and yet, I have still won.

I AM ALWAYS SAD

Darkness descending upon me, narrating my thoughts as it expands
Emptiness is eating me away, ignoring my own commands
Panic swallows me more than I can withstand
Reaching for something, someone, a helping hand
Emphasizing my pain so that you may understand
Soon it will consume me entirely as it always demands
Scared for myself, not knowing what it has planned
Imagining my death, thoughts I try to disband
Over and over again, my mind and heart are dragged
Not knowing that, in the end, I am indeed and utterly damned

In a cold, dark room, I sit alone
The thunderous rain picks up, matching my tone,
The deafening silence is broken by my phone

In a cold, dark room, I sit alone
Unlike the maddening mistakes, I can't disown,
The deafening silence is broken by my phone

My head humphs with a weight like a heavy stone,
In a cold, dark room, I sit alone
Each gust of wind lets out a wild groan.

The heaviness inside cuts to the bone,
The deafening silence is broken by my phone
In a cold, dark room, I sit alone

Until I can't take back, backspace, or delete,
My mind spirals out into the unknown,
The deafening silence is broken by my phone

In this doom and gloom is where I've grown,
In a cold, dark room, I sit alone
The deafening silence is broken by my phone

SUICIDE

It takes only a minute to decide.

Anger, sadness, and guilt coincide.
My hands reach for a blade to glide.

Seeking for the skin to collide
All the anger now subsides
Disbursing into more guilt as I suddenly realize

How do we know when moments turn into memories?
When friends suddenly turn into enemies
When coping turns into abuse and you need the high just to remedy

How do we know when the last time is the last?
Is it when we're haunted by the ghosts of our past
Or when every single friendship just doesn't seem to last

I'm struggling to comprehend
How this is my life when I tried so hard to amend
But broken things can't bend
And even though I have very few friends
I would have the few who are real rather than the plenty who pretend

ALONE

Fading away into the background as I become one with the unknown
Read the room as well as their tone
It seems to change as if I'm the one they've outgrown
Endless anxiety as I blend in with the trash they've thrown
Naivety plagues me as I try again, but they don't
Dear "friends," I'll still give you the kindness I was never shown
Learning that even if my heart is pure, others are made of stone
Emptiness and loneliness engulf me, keeping my mouth sewn
Surrounded by enemies who will still come to my tombstone
Sincerely, a girl who is forever on her own.

The Words I Couldn't Say

Dear abuser, harasser, and Mr. DM's bigger than the milky way,
The boy who cried wolf so he could catch his prey
The boy who choked me until the screams were blocked along my airway
The boy who could hang out on the weekend but never the weekday
The boy who I thought I could keep, praying I wasn't the one he would betray
The boy who promised me the world and stabbed my back, to my dismay
The boy was just a boy, but he was my boy, and he did not stay

Dear liar, deceiver, and fabricator
The girl who told her own stories so she would be perceived as greater
The girl who became so good at falsifying reality, practically an illustrator
The girl who stole the details of others and mimicked them like the perfect imitator
The girl who puppeteered other's actions because she was an instigator
The girl whose actions hurt more than any boy, a true violator
The girl who was just a girl, but was my girl, and she was a traitor

FURY

Listen last, speak first, my mind utters obscurely
Ending every friendship prematurely
The rage is all-consuming, and it wants all the glory

The lines suddenly become blurry.
Hate is the only emotion that assures me
Evenly matched with the heat of Mercury
Must justice always be extracted by a jury?

Bite my tongue to keep it from telling its own story
Until the bite turns bittersweet and every retched word comes up from the quarry
Regret pierces my heart, for my mind is the true bully
Now I sort through the damage, slowly, but surely

Do you know what betrayal feels like?
It's laying in bed wide awake with tear-stricken eyes at midnight
It's everything going right but feeling so wrong
It's consistent breakdowns alone because everyone tells you to "stay strong."
It's a lemon squeezed over a paper cut
It's the sinking feeling in your gut
It's smiling to your face but never behind your back
It's thinking you're sane, but people whispering "maniac,"
It's a tight hug that emphasizes cruelty, not warmth
It's a sunny day with lightning storms
It's being so excited only for someone to tell you you're being too loud
It's shutting down again because your dad was never proud
It's looking at your phone and realizing you're now blocked
It's opening your phone to a post of your "best friends" hanging out, leaving you shocked
Betrayal is the sinking feeling in your stomach
Right next to the butterflies that died all too quick

HIGH

Sadness is the emotion I use to dignify
Taking so many pills so I may nullify
Over and over again, I started to rely
Not wanting to remember, in need to occupy
Eager to feed the addiction, I cannot deny
Didn't anyone tell you that this is my goodbye?

Once invincible, now invisible
Formidable turned into despicable

The loudness was silenced
Aggression turning to violence

Smiles turned into frowns
There was no more happiness to be found

Jokes were made, but there was no more laughter
Once upon a time, with no happily ever after

Don't be so shocked
When it was her you mocked

I was told I lack vulnerability
You will need to forgive me
I lack it because of a father figure who was an absentee
Or maybe it's because of my family that offers no stability

1. Too loud to be in public, but when I'm quiet I'm "too depressing"
2. Too confrontational, but when I keep it to myself, I'm the problem for not addressing
3. Too stupid to actually know anything, so when I say something smart, I'm "just guessing"
4. Too worried about everyone's feelings, but when I'm finally calm, you make me feel guilty for no longer stressing
5. Too blunt, but when you want to know something, it's me your pressing
6. Too big-mouthed, but when you need information, its other's secrets you're confessing
7. Too much to myself, but I tell one story and now I'm too expressing
8. Too expressing because I tried to open up, but now it's a problem so I'm back to suppressing
9. Too much of a whore, but you had to wait til I wasn't sober so it could be me you were undressing
10. Too many friends, but it's only you I'm reassessing
11. Too toxic, but when I try to change, you claim there's no progressing

-*I can't do anything right, can I?*

I never cared much for my reputation.
People will always talk, no matter how miniscule the information.
So I'd speak my mind constantly, my actions backing up every conversation.
Eventually, actions turned into aggravation.
Words knew no violation.
Somewhere along the way, standing up for myself and saying everything I wanted, got lost in translation.
Hatred made me believe that it was only self-preservation, but all it led to was my own damnation.
Now I see that the two have no correlation.
I was the only one who led me into isolation.
I found myself with very few friends and blaming it on their lack of communication.
And maybe that was true, but if my reactions were any indication
Of weak-mindedness and hate narration
Then it's true, and people who I didn't know knew me and my every situation.
Situations I handled poorly and with great irritation.
Now they have a version of me they built off using their own inclination.

Am I a whore? I am not a whore.
　　　　　　　I am not a whore.　Am I a whore?
　　　　　　　I am not a whore.
Am I a whore?　I am not a whore.
　　　　　　　I am not a whore.
　　　　　　　I am not a whore.　Am I a whore?
　　　　　　　I am not a whore.
　　Am I a whore?　I am not a whore.
　　　　　　　I am not a whore.
　　　　　　　I am not a whore.　Am I a whore?
　　　　　　　I am not a whore.
Am I a whore?　I am not a whore.
　　　　　　　I am not a whore.　Am I a whore
　　　　　　　I am not a whore.
　　　　　　　I am not a whore.
　　Am I a whore?　I am not a whore.
　　　　　　　I am not a whore.
　　　　　　　I am not a whore.　Am I a whore?
Am I a whore?　I am not a whore.
　　　　　　　I am not a whore.
　　Am I a whore?　I am not a whore.
　　　　　　　I am not a whore.
　　　　　　　I am not a whore.
　　　　　　　I am not a whore.　Am I a whore?
　　　　　　　I am not a whore.
　　　　　　　I am not a whore.
　　　　　　　I am not a whore.
　　Am I a whore?　I am not a whore.
　　　　　　　I am not a whore.
　　　　　　　I am not a whore.　Am I a whore?
　　　　　　　I am not a whore.

The truth has two sides; even then, it is buried under emotions and pointed fingers.
The truth is a biased story told from lies that still linger.
The truth stopped becoming objective
Because being objective would mean that the side you're secretly on, doesn't favor the general perspective.
So, the truth became subjective.
And your lies became the new favorite collective

Nothing feels like it matters anymore
When you're drowning in your own sorrows and fighting your own war
Every road leads to a closed door
People might argue that taking your own life is a weak choice
But was it a strong choice for other people to take away her voice?
Pushing her to the edge of a burning building, but if she jumped, it was because she was weak.
Not because she was constantly harassed, told to kill herself, and driven to never speak.
It would be her fault that she got assaulted and abused
Because she was a whore and she never outright refused
But how could she when she was drugged and confused
Not that the world would care if she was misused
Who would miss someone who was always just sad
This time, just this time, she'll give them the upper hand.
She'll grab the pill bottle as planned.
Hoping that the few people who loved her might try to understand
It was the pain and the people she could no longer withstand.
That this was the only way left.
Deep down, she knew it was for the best.
It's not their fault her building was burning, even if they held the matches
She was always destined to lay in the ashes.
-Burned out

What will it take for someone to ask if she's okay?
Does she need to slice her wrists for them to beg her to stay?
Because It seems like acting out just drives people away.
She doesn't smoke, but she tried it anyway.
Then she tried again, hoping that with a new addiction, someone would have something to say.
But no one did, so she continued her old ways.
-I am not okay

Friends with benefits was always something she hated.
The feeling of being used and wanted, but never dated.
She thought at least this way; love was awaited.

But, just like every other guy,
There was no hey and certainly no hi.
Were they even friends anymore if she stopped receiving replies?
Just another mindless hookup that would end up in a good cry
And would only bring her closer to wanting to die

Oh, parking garage girl
Never the diamond, but still a pearl
Worth something, just not enough
Always promised flowers, dates, and other bluffs

Oh, parking garage girl
Won't he show you the world?
Why a dark place where no one can see your beautiful face?

Oh, parking garage girl
You are worth so much more
Than just a kiss in the dark
Won't you leave before it tears you apart?

Oh, parking garage girl
You miss who you were before
The mountain of empty promises and lies
Killed all the butterflies
And how she now realized
There was never love in his eyes
Just lust because she was only ever a prize

Oh, parking garage girl
You could be great on your own
Why won't you give it a whirl?

Oh, parking garage girl
Please don't be scared to try
For anything other than just a guy

Oh, parking garage girl
You are your own everything
Oh, parking garage girl
Not every queen needs a king
-*I love you*

I'd like to believe that I'm misunderstood
But maybe I'm just not inherently good.
Somewhere along the way, the heroine became the villain.
Trading secrets became a win-win
What I thought was the end was only the beginning

I MISS THE OLD ME

Cold to the touch, my warm heart is now a memory
Once okay, now bordering insanity
My younger self begging to come out, a sorrowful scream, a plea
Easily she loves, so I shoved her in captivity

Barricading her from myself because I am my own enemy
Afraid to live happily when all I know is misery
Control my thoughts as I try to grasp my reality
Knowing that my story was written to be a tragedy

Every time I think I've grown up, I'm right back at the kids table
Friendships match my behavior as they become unstable
And I have yet to realize this is no fable
There are no happy endings if I'm the one who is unable
To keep peace and stop expecting some savior
-*It's time to grow up*

I never really thought of myself as good enough for anyone
I had my insecurities, sure
Now it's different.
It's no longer my voice telling me I'm not good enough
It's yours

You, who made me believe I was amazing
Only to disappear and make me feel even worse than I did initially.

You, who saved me from myself
Only to drown me in the same pool full of sorrows you pulled me out of.

I know that I'm the one with the issues,
But why go to therapy when I can use tissues?
There are probably better ways to handle my problems rather than burning my flesh with freshly burned-out matches,
and to slice my skin open with a razor blade and blame it on cat scratches
But I prefer the decay and depression over conflict and confessions.
It's too much to feel, and too little do I heal
So when I burn my skin, I imagine it's my emotions I'm burning
And when I bleed from my blade, It's for a lesson I'm still learning
For feelings that won't quit returning and a broken heart that's still yearning
But it's the way I deserve to deal with it.
Not a pretty talk on a pretty couch where you sit and admit.
Not a nice discussion where I can't face any repercussions
I deserve to feel pain.
My heart and body are the same.
I deserve the burn and blood, every cut, every scar
Because a scar is still proof that I've made it this far
-*Help me*

Borderline Personality Disorder

When people hear the word disorder, they look at you like you're broken.
Before you've even spoken,
Or attempt to get an explanation out in the open,
They look at you like life has given them a bad omen.

And it's quite funny,
How you're the one who's diseased, and yet, they make you feel worse and crummy.

You didn't choose to live life this way.
Feeling too much every single second of the day.
Begging everyone to stay.
Shattering when they walk away.
Never knowing how to be okay.
Watching your life decay.
Always feeling betrayed.

There's nothing wrong with me.
At least nothing wrong that you can physically see.
Mentally, I wish I could be set free.
My brain is my worst enemy.
I push people away, and ask why they leave.

I don't know how to keep living.
I promise I keep giving and giving.
But life can be so unforgiving.
And it's never me that someone's missing.
That hurts more than all the terrible memories I'm constantly reliving.

The Last Straw

So, you wanna play the role of a back-stabber?
Only I don't think you're "playing", or that it's just a "role"
You want to treat me like I don't matter?
Prove that you're in control?

Let me clear the air,
I put distance between us because I still care
When it came down to it, you were the one not there.
Unless it was a new boy, then of course you might stop to stare.

You hung out with guys who've called me whores and pushed me to suicide.
You prioritized them like they were your best friend while you threw me aside.
I've told you how I felt repeatedly, but there was no change, so don't you dare tell me you tried.
What you did try to do was steal a guy from me, while claiming you never lied
How many more times should I feel disrespected before I need to decide?
The lack of self-awareness and your never-ending pride,
Will always leave you feeling alone and empty inside.

Hypocrite

When you hang out with my ex-friends,
I want you to remember how this friendship ends.

You chose to walk away.
I needed space, but I still stayed.
I'm glad that we're not friends today,
Because to see you act so two-faced
Was a blessing in disguise anyway.

When you look at the friends you hated and shit talked,
And always obsessively watched and stalked,
I hope you find yourself feeling miserable at that very thought.

You did not deserve to be the reason of my fallen ashes
And when your boy-obsessed phase passes,
And your're back to being a girls-girl
I will not be here for you anymore.

It got so bad, I stayed silent.
It was in my nature to defend so aggressively, I became violent.
But don't mistake my silence as compliance.
-*I won't give you the satisfaction of a reaction*

No one really prepares you for the feeling of heartbreak.
Not from a lover, but from a best friend masking her scales and slithering with the snakes.
But vipers did always camouflage until they bit and flaked.
Leaving you to your own poisoned wake.
It was truly my own mistake,
For confusing kindness, compassion, and love for jealousy and hate.
-*My mom was right about you*

EATING DISORDER

Stretch marks I look at in horror
Telling tales of my obesity, such torture
An image of what I could be becomes my only supporter
Ruining myself as my body screams bloody murder
Victory I can see at this very corner
Idling my body while my heart waits at the border
Numbers on the scale deceive, but who would warn her?
Gave in, my mind its own usurper

I talk a big game for someone who feels vacant
I've run out of anger and patience
So where do I go now?
I lost my friends again, but I don't know how.
When they wronged me, but still get to talk shit
Honestly, I just don't get it
-I also just don't seem to care.

The Venom of the Viper

You are a back-stabber.
Deny all you want, but as soon as I turned around, you threw your dagger.
A couple of times, for that matter.
A double-crosser and a double-dealer.
Make sure to add to your resume a "certified homewrecker" and "man-stealer"
Oh, and let's not forget a secret revealer.
A betrayer.
An onion with many rotten layers.
You are the Judas of the twenty-first century.
Your basic human decency being utterly rudimentary.
A venomous viper and a conniving turncoat.
Switching sides and swapping notes
With people I didn't like, just so you could gloat.
Fraternize and collude all you want,
I just hope your boyfriend doesn't find out about the many guys you talk to because you "feel too bad" to stop.
Male validation won't complete your traitorous heart.
And I'm sure since I'm not there to keep you in check, this is only the start.

The Final Countdown

What happens when all the anger is subsided
And all the flames are finally snuffed?

A lot of feelings were left undecided
Which, at the time, felt too tough

I know I should get my shit together and pick up the pieces I broke
But the anger was motivating me,
and there are no more emotions left to evoke

It's just empty and hollow
And I don't care
I just sit now and wallow
In feelings of misery and despair

I wish I had a dad that loved me
I wish I had a brother that never died unexpectedly
A father figure or older brother that was constant
Never disappeared or left a physical imprint
Instead I have people who make fun of the loss of my baby brother
And people who make me wish I had another
There are no boys in my life
And no situationships will ever suffice
I just want to be a part of a loving family
Not one filled with anger and misery
-dysfunctional didn't have to mean broken

When you look at me
What do you see?
Endless anxiety
Waiting to be set free
Clinging to you like you once did to me

Look up at the sky
Sit under a tree
Summers in July
If only you would agree
But you wanted to leave

I forget on purpose
Remember on accident
Memories resurface
All broken and bent

Will you help me up when I fall?
Or will you say goodbye at last
When things got hard, you got small
I'm sorry I even asked
Let me leave you in the past

But I didn't leave you, did I?
You left, and now you're dead
You thought I didn't try
But I can't dodge a gun that you loaded with lead
And neither could you, otherwise you'd be here instead

Sometimes, when the tears don't come
I need to watch a sad movie, or read a sad book
I've held up my sadness for ransom
Baiting it with a shiny hook

But I've mistaken shine for rust for far too long
They say opposites attract
So if I attract rust and everything that's inherently wrong,
Does that make me a shiny artifact?
Or have I been shining on my own all along?

I can never seem to sleep
No melatonin or counting sheep
Can lull me into a slumber so deep

Overthinking keeps me up at night
As well as in the daylight
It eats me alive and I can't even put up a fight
Because everything it shows me is right

So sometimes I take Nyquil when I'm not sick
And sometimes I take Benadryl because it's effective and quick
And maybe, that was always the trick

To tell myself I need it to go to bed
But really, it's to avoid everything going on in my head.

I'm in love with someone who doesn't love me back
I think that's the most brutal form of attack
You would think it was real after all this time
Making it all up was my only crime.

ANXIETY

Hands shaking violently
In spite of what everyone's telling me
Discussing problems and "breathing" is a trick taught by society
Everyone stares when I just want privacy

My head constantly shooting a million thoughts– an ongoing rivalry
Everlasting fear anchoring my body lifelessly

You deny the inevitable truth
That you used and discarded me like a faulty subscription.
I must say, that this is a different type of abuse
No physical slap or verbal insult could have caused me more affliction.
I wanted you,
You wanted to use me.
Why pretend to pursue?
Why would you give me hope knowing there was never going to be a we?
I confessed how I felt, and you are entitled to not feel the same way
But as soon as I say no to any of your favors, it's not okay?
You claimed to be a man, and yet act like any other frat boy cliche
Don't you get it?
For you, it was the end of the day
For me, it was the end of my world with my bleeding heart sitting on a display
We are not the same
-*I wanted it to be you, but you didn't*

I take meds instead of my life
I cut friends instead of my wrists
I light candles instead of my arms
I write apologies instead of goodbye letters
-*I'm learning*

I just want to be understood or heard
So, so badly that all of the lines are bloody and blurred
You can't see what's right and wrong with teardrops over your eyes
Will you hear my pleas if they come out in cries?
Pretending to be okay was my only disguise
-Are you listening?

Every now and then, I decide to give life another chance.
I give it my all, pouring more than my heart could withstand.
Now when the eyebags return worse than before,
And I feel even emptier and less sure
I know what needs to be done,
The sadness has finally won.

Happy Anniversary

They say that time heals trauma If that were true,
I would be dealing with new problems–not the same past drama
Two years later, and I'm still thinking about you
Time has passed, but your hands haven't untouched me
The trace of your unwanted fingers still haven't left the inside of my body
The taste you forced inside my mouth hasn't left my memory
Scars don't disappear instantaneously
But perhaps they will fade over time
Along with my body because you made sure it was never really mine
Allowing myself to think about what you did to me, even now, feels like the biggest crime
I bet you've never looked back once while my head is now constantly turned
And even after you, it happened over and over again so I guess the lesson was never really learned

Party of One

I know you're tired of hearing how sad I am
I'm tired of the sadness and loss of epigrams
I can take the hint
No more hangouts until I completely break and reconstruct the blueprint
Because no one likes the sad girl who can't have fun
But what they don't know is that the sad girl is just as done

Sitting in the passenger seat, looking out the window
My eyes catch a glimpse of a woman whose soul is stuck in limbo
What will she decide?
Will she take the pills to commit suicide?
It wouldn't be the first time that she tried
The last time she popped any pills was months ago
She was changing, slowly, but enough to grow
I want to tell her not to listen to them
This wasn't her anymore, she shouldn't be condemned
Yet they still call her an addict
How much more pain could they inflict?
I couldn't watch anymore
So I turned away from the side mirror and let my eyes fall to the floor
Because I know that I must be better than before
-I don't mind dying, but that doesn't mean I'll stop trying

If I change my persona to leave me alone,
At least I can say I chose to be lonely
Rather than being left alone
And wanting to be loved

Every time I choose to start over
Attempting to erase the sins of my past
I'll pick a new person like I pick a clover
And because I picked them, my favorite person doesn't seem to last

To be loved is to be seen

Would they understand me if I was portrayed on a movie screen?

Would they see me if I was who they wanted me to be?

-No, they wouldn't

Words are just words

Insane, unhinged, bat-shit crazy
Memories become uncertain and hazy

Words are just words

Whore, slut, tease, easy
Untrue, yet they make me feel so sleazy

Words are just words

Bitch, liar, problematic
Minding my business never felt so dramatic

Words are just words

Negative, suicidal, depressed
Please just give it a rest

Words are just words

Loud, obnoxious, violent
It's best if I stay silent

Words are just words

Words are just words until they're not
Words are just words until you get caught

Words are just words until they come alive
Words are just words until you commit suicide

My biggest fear is being forgotten
That people move on without me
Change is meant for roses not for the rotten
I bet they'll look happier with new memories
-How do I change without the anger of a fatherless daughter?

I don't have anything to offer anymore
I want to be so completely off the grid that I become unknown
I don't have anything to offer anymore
I'd kill my self, but I'm supposed to be all healed and grown
I don't have anything to offer anymore
Can I please just be left alone
I don't have anything to offer anymore
I really don't.

Threats of violence and death
No empty words or signs of regret
Headphones to hollow out the noise
Until the entire house is destroyed
The house was never a home anyway
Homes are filled with a love that stays

You can have a boyfriend who makes you smile
You can play pretend for a little while
But when he goes home
And you're all alone
Don't forget where you came from
The depression lingers outside, waiting for you to come

The Ballad of an Insane Girl

Loud, lethal screams surrounded the room,
Terrorizing throbs inside her maddening mind.
She screamed in answer, beckoning the bellow,
Begging, pleading—would they just be kind?

She aimed to confront the sharpening shouts.
But the noise deepened her fear to fight.
The echoes of screams intertwined with her cries,
Now, she could no longer tell if it was day or night.

Her wails rang out until they turned to whispers.
Muttering promises of silence and solitude.
The deafening darkness wrapped around her like chains,
Was there an end to this fatal feud?

Violent voices hounded her head,
Suffocating—until her voice carried no breath.
She couldn't fight what she couldn't see,
But facing the mirror, she knew her mind would be her death

It's mid-July
The grass is stained yellow, and the flowers have bloomed
I should turn on the sprinklers so they don't die
But maybe the seasons will change faster if no water is consumed

I start buying sweaters in summer
And wait for the animals to hibernate
It might seem like a bummer
But I simply cannot wait

I prepare for the future in anticipation of what's next
Until it's July again, and I haven't bought a new sweater
I'm left feeling anxious and perplexed
And I ask myself if this is better
Or if I should put it to rest

So now I enjoy the summer breeze
And I buy sweaters in the fall
Because waiting for the change in leaves
And chasing after ideas blocked by walls
Will make the wait worth less, and leave you never feeling pleased

I have some anger issues
I wrote it all down
I burned the letters along with your views

I had some anger issues
I changed my perspective
I'm doing better now that I'm no longer in your shoes

I had some anger issues
Sometimes they come back
But now, I don't blow the fuse

The Line

What is friendship if not unspoken rules?
Was it real love if you made me look like a fool?
To pour my heart out and open up
Only to realize you never held out a cup
To tear my walls down and love all my flaws
Just for you to break me and follow it with a round of applause

Time goes on, but I stay still
Friendships are hard to form because the real me died on that hill
The same place you left me scarred and burned
Surface level, like all my relationships, now that you've become a lesson I learned
I moved on physically, but the rest of me is still there
My heart is closed off, the pain too much to bear

Eventually, your pain will fade away
I won't be afraid to be myself or stay
I'll love the next person more than my fear
I'll be able to love, but you'll still be here
You taught me a lesson, and now I know the signs
And though I'll be okay, you'll always be the line.

Sorrows at Sea

When the night is still and silent
And the waves are no longer vicious or violent
A soothing calmness sets in
And you stare as the chill of the wind kisses your skin
Every breath feels fresh and free
The ocean stares back as if it agrees

The ache in your bones needs to be suffocated or quenched
The relentless urge to flee, but your heart feels drenched
Drowning in a sea of sadness and endless consistency
With an unspoken wish to run away or leave

The ice-cold water washes over your feet
And the feelings of freezing and freeing start to compete
The salty air lifts the sand and blows it away
Each grain of sand will leave, but not you; you'll stay
After all, you and the vast blue ocean are one and the same
Reflecting calmness and chaos but only having yourself to blame

Everything sucks
But, it will be okay.

The End

www.ingramcontent.com/pod-product-compliance
Lightning Source LLC
Chambersburg PA
CBHW031656040426
42453CB00006B/325